A Sequel to
I am With You

MY BURDEN
IS LIGHT

**Treasured words of divine
inspiration as given to
Fr John Woolley**

T0169046

First published by New Life Publishing,
Luton, Bedfordshire LU4 9HG
Printed 2006, extended 2009,
reprinted 2010 and 2012

This edition by Circle Books, 2015
Circle Books is an imprint of John Hunt Publishing Ltd.,
Laurel House, Station Approach, Alresford, Hants, SO24 9JH, UK
office1@jhpbooks.net
www.johnhuntpublishing.com
www.circle-books.com

For distributor details and how to order please visit the 'Ordering'
section on our website.

Text copyright: John Woolley 2006
ISBN: 978 1 78279 597 1

A CIP catalogue record for this book is available from the
British Library.

Scripture quotations are taken from various translations

Printed in the USA by Edwards Brothers Malloy

A Sequel to
I am With You

MY BURDEN
IS LIGHT

**Treasured words of divine
inspiration as given to
Fr John Woolley**

Winchester, UK
Washington, USA

Introduction

Following the establishment of the much-loved devotional book *I Am With You*, now in constant use throughout the world, further inspiring words (received from our Lord in times of prayer by Fr. John Woolley) are contained in this new volume, *My Burden is Light*.

The life-changing and peace-giving words of the risen Lord Jesus, through His Holy Spirit, are certain to be experienced in this latest companion to *I Am with You*.

The Christian road is often far from easy. What *My Burden is Light* provides is unique help in learning to be calm and strong in very difficult circumstances, and in finding Jesus our Lord a lifelong tower of strength.

As our Lord's word is received, we discover increasingly, that we have a wonderful Friend!

I know that our Lord will speak to you through the pages of this book. I have prayed that many burdens will be lifted - including those existing for a long time.

Please be unhurried as you dwell carefully on each page. We can feel that we are coming to the true source of peace in this uncertain world.

May the Lord Jesus (God the Father with us) bless every moment that you spend in His word.

John Woolley

My child, from the outset I accepted the burden of a fallen world in order to bear pain for My children.

My purpose, always, is to bring, through My sharing, a knowledge of My love which otherwise would not be there.

As you look at the Cross, see the Creator's willing acceptance of the pain in creation.

Think of the sharing which followed as not merely for the world, but for individuals, as each child, through My own suffering, comes to find hope.

God so loved the world...
(John 3: 16)

1

ANY turning to Myself is always, firstly, to Calvary, where My love most readily can be seen.

It is here that I take from you the burdens of fear, and of self-blame, and it is here that the basis of love is established for our permanent relationship.

My child, my *love* dictates that I cannot look upon you as bowed down with cares of many kinds.

My *victory* ensures that I can take your burdens into Myself, and can then prevent evil from troubling your spirit.

**For the sake of my sheep
I surrender My life**
(John 10: 15)

2

$\mathcal{M}$Y child, not for one moment have you suffered alone, because I truly have upheld you.

My own heart has been deeply hurt by all your experiences of life's pain.

The cost of My sharing in humanity - seen at Calvary... this *involvement* will never fail you.

Do you see that My love is hurt whenever you are burdened? This is why I always desire to lift burdens for you.

The world has still to appreciate the depth of My love.

I am the Good Shepherd
(John 10: 14)

*A*s you gaze at the Cross frequently through your life, no question need ever arise about My willingness to bear everything which, in your weakness, you cannot bear.

Having watched, with Me, at Calvary, you can then contemplate the same love enfolding you now... an enfolding which enables you to be the *child* I always see.

My child, never cease to be grateful that in a world with so many trials you possess Me!

There is no greater love than when a person lays down his life for his friends
(John 15:13)

SO much needless pain results
from not accepting My invitation
and not allowing Me to bear
anxiety, sadness and guilt for you.

My child, always remember that it
gives joy to My heart when I am
able to shoulder a burden which is
proving too much for you. It
becomes yet another instance of My
love's desire being *fulfilled* ...

Whenever you whisper My name
helplessly, it is always a sign that
the bond between us is unbroken.

As that helpless child, wrapped
around by My love, you are then
truly able to *receive*.

**Unless you become
like children**
(Matthew 18: 3)

5

MY child, I have made clear to you that the only condition for your being free of life's burdens is to accept the light 'burden' of merely loving Me and serving Me!

My child, do not underestimate how much your own trust and your attentiveness towards Me is able to lift *My* burden of sorrow over My world.   In this way, we are carrying for each other - which constitutes a *true* friendship.

My child, never weary in trusting Me!

My yoke is easy
(Matthew 11:30)

*T*HE essential relationship between your creator and yourself is that of Father and child. In various ways, allow yourself to *be* that child... in your thinking, and in the simplicity of your actions.

The more a child submits to My love, (resting in it) the more sure will be that child's walk with Me at all other times.

As you bring your burdens to Me, you can take for granted My lifting of those burdens because My love can do no other!

Do not try to 'feel' the sense of your burdens being lifted; instead, simply thank Me, in sheer trust, that all has been taken into My love.

Whatever you ask in prayer, believe that you have it, and it will be so
(Mark 11:24)

WHEN you feel completely unequal to your situation, do not attempt anything except simply throwing yourself upon Me.

Do not be hurried. Remain there, in My arms, until My peace begins its work in your heart.

My child, I again emphasise to you that you are not meant to bear the burdens which life produces, and which are My responsibility.

Whenever you surrender a situation to my working, I want you to instantaneously feel My shouldering of that which you have given to me.

Come to me ...
(Matthew 11: 28)

I want you to know that if you keep very close to Me during any time of great testing, I *hold* you.

I hold you so that you do not break under the forces which are at work.

Just keep Me there until the storm begins to subside, as it always will.

Always remember the analogy with an earthly parent and child.

I am there, like a good parent, to do for you what you are unable to do for yourself, supporting your faltering steps.

I am able to carry you
(Isaiah 46: 4)

$\mathcal{M}$Y child, if only you were able to see the road ahead which you have chosen to tread with Me!

You would see how that road differs from all the other roads of life. My road has far fewer obstacles compared with others because many of them (temptations, discouragements, opposition), have already been removed for you.

The obstacles remaining are there to prove your trust in overcoming, and are in no way wasteful, as are so many of the hazards of earth.

I am the Way
(John 14: 6)

WHAT I desire for you is a *permanent* state of being unburdened!

This will happen for you as my love fills your consciousness increasingly, and the sense of your having a Companion on life's road becomes instinctive.

This will mean that whenever you are aware of a burden of the spirit recurring, then you will (almost unthinkingly!) simply return it into My hands.

You will find rest for your soul
(Matthew 11: 29)

*T*HE way in which the bearing of your burdens takes place is essentially an *interior* one...

Deep within your spirit My own spirit is enlarged and the weight which you carry is lifted.

In place of the burden I bequeath to you tranquillity, and the sure hope of My perfect solution.

My child, Yes, I do have *all* possibilities within My control. I will *only* permit what I see is best for your life. Are you content that this is so?

Not only My bearing of your every burden, but My carrying of *you*.

Peace which the world cannot give
(John 14: 27)

My child, so often it will be difficult to see beyond the darkness.

The starting point for your recovery is reminding yourself of something which you may temporarily have forgotten... that you have *Me!*

Increasingly, that quiet assurance that you possess Me will mean that nothing else in existence really matters!

Remember that evil forces will attempt to lie to you but as you look earnestly for Me, the peace of My love in you is utterly secure.

The Son of Righteousness will rise upon you with healing in His wings
(Malachi 4: 2)

γOU may often feel that you simply cannot go on.

It is at such times that I bless even the very slightest effort which you then bring yourself to make, after seeking My strength.

Simply being what you could not be without Me!

If there is one place, above all others, where you must never lose heart, it is when you are upon My road.

My child, you surely have found that when every aspect of life is uncertain there is a place of absolute stability... the *rock* which is your Saviour and Friend.

In your weakness, My strength is made perfect
(2 Corinthians 12: 9)

MY child, when you tell Me that you feel afraid, even the very sharing with Me begins to lessen the fear which you feel!

Let there be times, often, when you cease all thought and all anxiety and *allow* My love's light to bathe you, resting in My strengthening arms.

Do not let such occasions be restricted to crisis periods! Just let receiving be an indispensable part of *every* day.

In your times apart with Me, I want you to feel yourself sinking deeper and deeper into My love!

I am with you to save you
(Jeremiah 1:19)

$\mathcal{M}$Y child, remember to frequently say the trusting words, 'In Your hands'.

This is both a statement of truth, and a bringer of peace.

Never doubt the continuing nature of My working for you - both within your heart and in those complexities of existence which so often cause you to despair.

As always, your expressions of trust in My providential care brings comfort to My heart.

**Blessed is he who
trusts in the Lord**
(Psalm 16: 20)

MY child, for you it must be *a walk in My love* - with that love dominant, and lighting up even the most disturbing elements of life.

My going before you in anticipation of each possible need.

My carrying of your burdens is so that you may be unrestricted in your relationship with Me, so that you may enjoy a real sense of freedom and so that you may *achieve* where previously you have been defeated.

My child, My burden-bearing is, in effect, giving you *permission to live*.

If I set you free, you are free indeed
(John 8: 36)

*T*HERE is always danger when the unity within the Godhead is forgotten.

Your devotion is weakened when the one-ness of the Father and the Son is in any way diminished, as is so often the case with those who endeavour to follow Me.

My child, the look to My love truly is a look to the love of the Father. As 'Lord', I am simply your Father or your Saviour, according to your need. The tenderness of My love must always show you, beyond all doubt, the tenderness of the Father's love.

I and the Father are one
(John 10: 30)

My child, do you look upon your present life as barren in worldly terms?

Is there much which you are tempted to envy in others?

In spite of these things, are you sure of My love for you?

Are you conscious of being My chosen?

Then you can thank Me that truly you are greatly blessed!

What profit is there in gaining the whole world?
(Mark 8: 36)

MY child, make sure that one part of your thinking never changes...

...that I can work upon any circumstance to turn it to good!

When you entrust circumstances to Me, it will not merely be a case of My not disappointing you.

Rather, it will be My giving you far more than you could have expected, as the response to your trusting Me!

I always wish to bless you abundantly, irrespective of what you feel you deserve.

A good measure, pressed down, shaken together and running over ... will be poured into your lap
(Luke 6:38)

My child, have you found that by letting your mind dwell upon My love, all the causes of anxiety and fretfulness are *automatically* seen in its light?

This is the transforming power, the *gentle* power of My love's radiance!

My child, let your spirit rise up into love's domain by simply taking Me at My word when I tell you 'I have loved you with an everlasting love'.

Let your spirit find true peace in that love *now*...

Such peace always rests upon My *faithfulness*.

I will not leave you without My comforting presence
(John 14:18)

MY child, firstly your
recognition of the ultimate loss ...
to be without me.

And then, your thankfulness for
two simple truths:

...in Me you have all that you need.
...in Me you have victory in all
   things.

You need to have only *one* fear...
that of losing My companionship.

I am pledged to respond to your
trust by an increasing sense, for you,
of love's covering, and the eventual
removal of all fear.

Without Me, you can do nothing
(John: 15: 5)

*T*HE great mystery of our relationship is that as your knowledge of Me grows so does your *need* of Me!

Therefore, My child, never be downcast at the thought of how very much you need Me, because this is a sign of *growth*.

Can you not see that acquaintance with Myself does not lessen your dependency on Me but actually increases it?

The needs of those in the world around you are always best met through a child who depends on Me for everything.

My God will meet all your needs according to His glorious riches in Christ Jesus
(Philippians 4:19)

*W*HEN circumstances cause you to cry out desperately to Me, that is when I draw very close to minister My love to you, above all.

The number of times that you cry out to Me in this way need not make you anxious! Each one is made a source of blessing to you.

My child, your look into My love and your ability to be victorious in all things: these two are simultaneous.

Never feel that you are wearing out my patience in your desperation. These are simply opportunities for the sense of My love to blend with that sense of need.

Much is made right for you by this alone.

It is I, do not be afraid
(Mark 10: 50)

*W*HEN there is a sense of desperation, it is always wisdom to come to Me *first*.

My child, let this always precede the natural seeking of consolation and understanding from human sources.

An instinctive turning!

Let Me quieten your spirit as I give to you what no other source can give. Then, unhurriedly, bring to Me, for My blessing, the approach you may make to any other child of Mine.

Yes, by making Me your first resort, an original intention to seek a source of human help may be made unnecessary.

Wait upon me
(Isaiah 55: 3)

25

MY children who share life with Me increasingly find something of Myself in the very darkest places.

  ... surprising kindnesses from sources least expected.
  ... being used, (in spite of the darkness) to bring Me to others at very critical moments in their lives.
  ... a little courage which you never thought could be in you.

Each time of our sharing means that there is now a little more of Myself in you!

It is all part of love's design, in which your hope need never die.

I can do all things through Christ who strengthens me
(Philippians 4: 13)

MY child, does your mind turn instinctively from observing all that is good in your world to the One who conceived it all, in love?

It is all part of having Me as the home of your thoughts!

Turning to myself as your friend from the frequent barrenness of life is rewarded by My blessing what is good in life's experiences.

Life's most precious moments are even more precious to you whenever their *source* is remembered.

Let your true satisfaction be in knowing Me
(Jeremiah 9: 24)

MY child, do you wish to find a sure way in which your love for Me will grow?

Is that desire strong?

Then, be sure to develop that sense of *gratitude* for My carrying all that would be unbearable of life's demands.

Gratitude for My unfailing accessability.

Gratitude for the priceless contrast between the 'burdened' you and the child whom I now carry.

Gratitude simply for *My* presence in your life.

Even the hairs of your head are all counted
(Luke 12: 7)

ALWAYS remember that in temporary disappointment there is something from which I am saving you.

My child, have in your mind always that I only allow circumstances which can be steps to heaven for you.

That is why you must summon up all your trust in seeing those circumstances as something for which you can thank Me - even if not immediately apparent to you.

**My thoughts are not
your thoughts**
(Isaiah 55: 8)

MY child, regret nothing that you feel you have missed in life, thus far.

I will always more than make up for everything as you are careful to consciously dwell in My love.

I will never be denied in My desire to bless a child who trusts Me, at whatever stage of his or her life.

You know that you have all eternity to enjoy what I see as important for you.

Any blessings will be so much more satisfying after the delays and deprivations.

I Myself am your wealth!
(Numbers 18: 20)

MY touch of love ...

... reaching you through many agencies, especially those I have commissioned for this purpose.

Do not be concerned about the particular *source* of the love which comes to raise your spirits. Simply thank Me that, in some way, I reached into your heart when I saw the need.

A human channel of the divine love will so often be one which you least expect!

I so often wonderfully use what the world considers 'weak'.

The Lord your God is faithful
(Deuteronomy 7: 9)

MY child, are you trusting My love more than ever before? It is wisdom to trust in this extravagant way because My love proves, ultimately, to be the answer to everything.

My child, you know that every concern of yours is My concern.

This is a completeness which can only be found in Myself.

No barriers erected by evil can keep out My love from the heart of a child who desires to know that love. That is the one desire which must *never* die.

Whoever drinks the water which I give will never thirst
(John 4:14)

$\mathcal{A}$RE you over-concerned about My answers to your prayers being seemingly delayed?

Do you question My working - especially in things very near to your heart?

It is in these circumstances that you must, at all costs, resist doubt of My *Person*, even if My ways may be hard to understand.

All that you have experienced of Me must convince you that I would not fail you in your *real* need.

With whom will you compare Me?
(Isaiah 40: 25)

*T*HE hands which are offered to you are sharing hands:

...sharing My understanding.
...sharing My goodness in so many
    ways.
...sharing My strength for your
    conquest of temptation.
...sharing My protection... (the
    universal shielding).
...sharing My caressing love.
...sharing My peace.

Yes, My child, nothing is held back from you which would help you to negotiate this present world.

**I will satisfy My people
with My goodness**
(Jeremiah 31: 14)

WHOEVER may be the subject of your prayer, be sure to ask for the dawning of My love in that person's heart.

This is the one request which I am pledged to fulfil. You can ask nothing more vital on behalf of another child... *to know My love.*

I can foresee a multitude of My children eventually coming to know My love!

My child, your prayer for a particular child of Mine hastens the fulfilment of My universal wish.

Blessed are the peacemakers
(Matthew 5: 9)

*T*O see clearly every issue which life presents, always see these issues through Myself, the reflection of truth.

In effect, seeing the world through My eyes - a grace which I grant to you.

Let My light show up everything worthless, everything which may spell danger.

My promise is that if I am used in this way, your path will be a secure one. The brief time spent as I reveal truth will be more than amply repaid.

Needless to say, one great benefit is that of time saved!

I will guide and instruct you
(Psalm 32: 8)

MY child, keep in your mind
the occasions on which I *receive* from
you. I *always* receive when you step
aside from the world, even just to
think of Me.

I *always* receive when you picture
the Cross, and allow it to enlarge
My place in your heart.

I *always* receive when you allow My
love to flow through you to another
child of Mine - even if only a smile,
or a gentle word of understanding.

I *always* receive when you choose
My road instead of a road which
seems so much easier, but which
sounds a warning in your heart.

And I *always* receive when you
come to Me for help!

**I have eagerly desired
to eat with you**
(Luke 22: 15)

MY child, when a dark world causes you to suffer, just come close in gentleness to warm My own broken heart over that world.

As always, whispering My name...

...you may not have suspected how much it means to Me as you draw close when experiencing life's pain.

Yes, this is the great mystery of our relationship.

Always let Me caress you in times of distress, knowing that your unconscious part is that of *giving* to Me.

**My soul is overwhelmed
with sorrow**
(Matthew 26: 38)

REMEMBER the *passing* nature of the difficulties we encounter, and do not let evil distort events to produce fear.

As I have made clear to you, you are always wise to see the power of evil at work in all distressing human situations. Just capitulate to My *love* when the pressures against you threaten to be too strong.

Finally, My child, a word to encourage you:

The reason why I promise not to fail you is that I know you will never turn away from Me!

**I will fear no evil,
for You are with me**
(Psalm 23: 4)

$\mathcal{A}$SK yourself why so many of My children have experienced a surprising turn of events in their favour when everything seemed to be ranged against them. This is because strength in a demanding situation, or meeting with others, lay on *their* side!

You must therefore go into every encounter conscious of My all-sufficient presence. You go with a covering of love and of that love's empowering.

The outcome of everything which we meet together lies in what I have told you... My faithfulness.

No-one will be able to stand up against you
(Joshua 1: 5)

*T*HE discipline of standing back..

My child, at last, do let *Me* carry out the many things after which you strive.

As you exercise restraint, you truly can thank Me for what I am doing, with a peace in your heart. All is part of My burden-bearing promise to you.

My child, you know that not a single aspect of your life is untouched by Me. Do not in any way restrict this all-embracing influence.

Yes, I am answering your prayers in the *best possible* way, as My love becomes more and more precious to you.

Consider the lilies of the field
(Matthew 6:28)

*F*REQUENTLY envisage My *enfolding*, with absolutely nothing contrary to your true well-being able to harm you.

There are so many moments when merely to be in the Refuge, receiving My peace, is all that matters!

My child, you can be sure that it will always be My *love's* answer to your prayers which will reach you!

My child, am I more and more in your thoughts?

Then the result can only be an instinctive carrying out of My will!

Be faithful unto death
(Revelation 2: 10)

$\mathcal{H}$AVE you *allowed* Me to grant you a totally unburdened existence in My love?

If this is so, there will be many times when you can, with your mind's eye, actually picture My bearing the burden of *everything* for you.

This visualisation represents reality. Yes, My will is that a precious child is no longer weighed down with the troubling of the spirit which emanates from the power of darkness.

My child, have you realised that giving Me your attention is more precious to Me than you could imagine?

**Praise be to the Lord,
who daily bears our burdens**
(Psalm 68: 19))

43

MY child, what is the most desirable situation for you?

Quite irrespective of external circumstances, the ideal state is one in which *every* strand of your life is pervaded by My love's influence.

Desire that ideal state with all your heart ... My love to be *everything!*

Truly you can anticipate the many wonderful things which will then be brought about.

Turn to Me with all your heart
(Joel 2: 12)

'SURRENDER' always means that the right road to follow will either light up in your heart, or will be revealed by events.

It is *My* work to ensure that what is for your eternal destiny is brought about.

You can therefore *accept* life's events once you have given all into My hands with your whole heart. You can be fully assured that I will let nothing go astray, even if life may appear to be threatening.

My child, how much *easier* is the state of surrender!

I hold you by your right hand
(Isaiah 41:13)

A life consciously lived in My company is the only true life.

Your sharing life with Me becomes one more place in your world where My redeeming work is carried out.

My kingdom is being extended through you - not so much by your intention, but merely by My presence, wherever you are.

The changes which you long to see in others need to be deep-seated, and are essentially *My* work, rather than the result of your striving. It is here that your *prayers* make the decisive difference.

Your prayers convey your intention but with *My* facilitating.

**I am the vine;
you are the branches**
(John 15:5)

*I*NCOMPLETE reliance upon Myself causes you to lose so much peace.

Let *Me* help you to loosen your own hold upon situations, giving Me greater freedom than ever in which to work.

You will need to ask yourself frequently whether I really do have all things in My hands.

As you believe this truth with all your heart, your ability to show great patience and restraint will become easier for you.

There is nothing in creation which is outside the change-making influence of My love.

All power in heaven and earth belongs to Me
(Matthew 28:18)

*Y*OU know that it is relatively easy to have a certain lightness of heart when life is, on the whole, kind.

But, for the child who really trusts Me, I grant an unburdened spirit even when there is much which would daunt you or oppress you.

As it discovers that burdens can be lifted in this way the world will be drawn to Myself, realising that I am able to give what others cannot!

Lightness of heart in spite of threatening circumstances is something I grant which is quite beyond price.

In quietness and in confidence shall be your strength
(Isaiah 30:15)

MY love at work!

My child, can you not see it?

Do not hinder that working by

   Impatience
   Striving
   Human 'cleverness'
   Trusting in your own efforts...
...rather than in My sufficiency

Keep in your mind that only *My* solutions are perfect.

Already you will have noticed that your obedience (though far from perfect), always ensures My *provision* in so many ways.

**Enter through the
narrow gate**
(Matthew 7:13)

$\mathcal{D}$ISTURBANCE of spirit can be caused both by painful present circumstances and by memories equally painful.

I have provided for you to look away from whatever distresses you, and to look, instead, into My countenance.   I wish this change of focus from darkness to light to become natural for you.

My child, you are learning that My love always carries peace with it. The more you give yourself to My love, *(casting yourself upon it)* the less troubled will be your spirit by any matter.

If only you had known what would bring you peace...
(Luke 19:42)

MY child, use the time when the temptation to despair is very great to look *only* at My promises to you.

Bring against the despair My promise, above all, that present sorrow *will* be turned into joy for you.

It is of the nature of *real* trust when you believe the best of Me, that a situation is receiving My attention with no tangible sign to believe this is so.

My child, if this is where you are at present, still express your trust, knowing that it will be fully justified.

**The Lord is faithful
to all His promises**
(Psalm 145: 13)

*T*O be the new person whom I foresaw when choosing you carries a certain urgency.

Constantly examine, in the searching light of My love, those attitudes which you sense are of the old self and, in My love's light, turn away from them.

As always, that turning-away is lovingly assisted.

What would have seemed utterly impossible without Me becomes achievable with your newfound strength!

Happy are those with pure hearts
(Matthew 5:8)

MY child, relinquishing your hold upon a burdensome situation as I work, may not, at first, be easy for you.

You know that I will be at work for you *in any event*, but, by your restraint, let it be the widest possible area for My working.

'Letting go' is what you will always be called upon to do...

'Letting go' where a matter seems insoluble...
'Letting go' when tempted to anger or persuasion...
'Letting go' when desiring hasty reconciliation...

You will never regret the handing to Me!

The birds, who do not sow, are fed by your heavenly Father
(Matthew 6:26)

SO many things can come between us ... used by evil to draw you away from Me. Because evil's main objective is to divide us, make sure that you have a desperate desire for closeness to Me.   I honour that desire by ensuring that evil does *not* succeed in any wooing of your heart.

Your frequent communion with Me establishes a *shield*. All troubling of the spirit can threaten to temporarily come between us. You can, therefore, see why I wish you to be free of all burdens, in that life of constant surrender.

Protect them from the evil one ...
(John 17:15)

*W*HEN there is great confusion, let the light of My love shine upon all, as I steady you.

Let My love's light shine through each circumstance before responding to it. This will make the crucial difference to the nature of your response, as (very deliberately) you rest in My love.

My child, never believe the lie that by giving Me your attention, something of importance is being neglected. Peace is ensured by lifting up everything to Me.

Very frequently!

The light shines in the darkness
(John 1:5)

MY child, realise that fear will always be a temptation for you.

In the realm of *thought*: Always resist fear by turning to My love and experiencing a simultaneous victory in that turning (a quiet victory, perhaps, but still a victory).

In the realm of *choices*: Do not assist evil by choosing to act out of either guilty fear or timid fear especially when the sense of My love is unclouded.

Defy evil, as it attempts (as it always will) to work through fear, because fear can so easily be established as a habit.

If a course of action carries no awareness that it would hurt Me, act courageously... with My love's permission!

Be strong, for I accompany you!
(Haggai 2:4)

MY child, do you desperately wish to please Me?

If that desire is there, I will always let you see *truth*.

You are aware that life has many deceptions, one of which is self-deception. Do not, therefore, temporarily put truth aside in telling yourself that a thing is other than it is.

If you are always careful to speak truth, you can then take for granted that My influence will be upon all difficult decisions.

If truth is distorted, the outcome could so easily be that which is not of Me, and which drastically holds up your life's progress.

All who love the truth are my followers
(John 18:37)

MY child, throughout your life I have borne so much that would have broken you down completely.

This is the divine privilege.

I know that you realise, thankfully, My *constant* work on your behalf, of which burden-bearing is one small part.

As you begin to find the true rest of soul which I promised, you will cease to expect too much of earthly agencies - none of which can give you the sense of security which you experience when trusting My *infallibility*.

Look to Me ... and be saved
Isaiah 45: 22)

MY child, are you rigorously refusing to let anything (however 'desirable') supplant me in your affections?

Many examples of human affection *are* pleasing to Me, simply because love is present. But let the *source* of all love be at the very centre of your life, because this constitutes your *safety*.

Safety, because the divine love will not falter as do even the strongest of human affections.

The divine love stands ready to fill the vacuum left by the loss of human sources.

I must always be in first place
(Exodus 20:3)

*A*s you have found, trusting Me
does not take away your awareness
of life's difficulties pressing upon
you. But these things are kept
within bounds as you deliberately
see each one against the background
of My love.

My love a *transforming* light, to
assure you that none of these things
can affect your walk with Me!

My child, your only place of real
safety is hidden in the arms of Him
who has creation as His *possession*.

Never doubt, as you contemplate
existence, the *resources* which are at
My command for you.

**All things were created
by Him and for Him**
(Colossians 1: 6)

*A*LTHOUGH My creative processes are so often gradual, the changes in your own heart *can* be instantaneous!

As you respond spontaneously and wholeheartedly to My love's invitation, even the *slightest* movement of your spirit towards Myself draws out My loving response.

That response shows itself in the calming of all that may be troubling you by enabling you to *rise above* these things.

With Me as your companion these changes of the heart become a permanent characteristic of your personality.

Follow Me!
(Matthew 4:19)

*T*HE physical and mental weariness which comes with the passing of the years is more than compensated for if you are My follower.

There comes into your life, as My gift, a wonderful sense of security, and of real hope, which is only to be found in Me.

My child reflect often on the truth that as long as you have Me in your life you have nothing at all to fear.

Truly you find a degree of *independence* from limiting factors such as age and environment.

My spirit will never leave you
(Isaiah 59:21)

MY child, never depart from the sure belief that evil *will not prevail*.

Frequently, picture My all-embracing *control*, with all that is of evil subject to Me.

My moulding of events is, therefore, certain. Allow this with every fibre of your being.

When you are very earnestly trying to walk in My way, realise that there is nothing but love between us.

You realise, also, that I will therefore bring about *exactly* what is right on your behalf.

**Your Father knows
what you need**
(Matthew 6:8)

MY child, as I take the weight of your burdens, a walk stretches ahead which you will negotiate with a trust and a courageous joy which may have seemed impossible for you.

All that you have learned will have shown you that you can leave the future *entirely* to My disposing.

This bequeathing to Me of what lies ahead will mean that the future is lit up for you and productive of a sense of *eager expectation*.

Do not be concerned about tomorrow
(Matthew 6:34)

MY child, let Me make you aware of the *gains* you have made.

Think *only* of these, because this is your assurance of further victories.

Wait on Me and I will show you not one recent gain, but many!

My child, how can you ever doubt My love? How can you ever doubt its working?

I know that My love means more and more to you, and that is why you will experience its *power* to affect, for good, every aspect of your life.

Be of good courage
(John 16: 33))

*R*EMEMBER that the temporary clouding of the sense of My love when you are thinking or acting contrary to My Spirit in you does not mean that My love towards you has in any way changed.

It is merely in the nature of a warning that it would be wise to examine present intentions or courses of action and to seek the restoration of harmony between us at all costs.

Let love have its way!

Return to me ...
(Isaiah 44:22)

*D*O not welcome anything to meet the need of the moment which you sense is not of Me, and is only transient in its value.

Never create for yourself a dependency which excludes Me.

My child, it is not always easy for you to wait upon Me patiently, but whenever you look to Me *alone* I will always rescue you.

Often a hard road, but the paths of the world always so much harder.

Make this rule for yourself: passing needs are only to be met by *what is of Me.*

Pruning you ...
(John 15:2)

$\mathcal{Y}$OU are aware that creation is vast, and largely inscrutable to the human mind.

My incarnation was to reveal the divine *love* as being all that you really need to know with certainty.

My child, how lost you would be amid the world's complexities without Me!...

Never fail to thank Me for the crucial difference which My presence makes to your life.

This need never be a formal expression of gratitude, but one of warmth, as you remember that in Me you have life's one priceless gift.

**I came to search for the lost
and to save them**
(Luke 19:10)

ONCE a matter has been given to Me, never doubt that there will be an *intervention*, on your own or on someone else's behalf according to My wisdom.

But the *time* of My loving, intervening will always be determined by My overwhelming concern for you.

Always be sure to ask that I will either prosper or over-rule whatever you may be led to say or do in burdensome circumstances given to Me. Never force when a way does not easily open.

My child, as always, patience.

**According to your faith,
may it happen for you**
(Matthew 9:29)

*A*LL circumstances are being made to serve the divine plan for your life, because you have given those circumstances to Me.

My child, remind yourself frequently of My plan unfolding, and you then will more easily find joy in surrendering.

Welcome My restraining hand in guiding you gently along the only sure road to heaven.

It is the hand of the Good Shepherd, anxious that a precious sheep does not run into danger.

From My path, look up *only* at He who is leading you.

My sheep listen to My voice ...
... and follow Me
(John 10:27)

MY child, do you realise that
My love is a constant thread
through each fluctuating
circumstance, simply because
you have welcomed that love?

Do you also realise that the
presence of My love changes the
character of each circumstance
(a change which is undetected by
the world around you)?

Situations can now become
favourable to you, which at first
they promised not to be. Love's
power!

See, I am doing a new thing
(Isaiah 43:19)

*T*HE creative power of the universe is precisely the same power which is channelled for the individual need of My children.

This knowledge will always help you to trust My *invincibility*.

When evil attempts to drive you into states of mind and spirit which would weaken your hold upon Me, remember your resources!

All that is needed for My power to prevail is your constant *openness* to Me. Because power resides in love, My victory over evil forces is beyond all dispute.

My child, frequently remember that victory as being yours.

**Thanks be to God
who gives us the victory
through our Lord Jesus Christ**
(1 Corinthians 15: 57)

SO often your situation will be such that you can only throw your-self upon Me! Taking refuge in Me, you then allow Me to take *yourself* and your *circumstances* into My love.

I always count it as the greatest *privilege* to ease the burdens of My children. As I have told you, this process began when, in love, I took mankind's sin upon Myself.

You can always take refuge in the thought of the Cross and in what that *sharing* love means for you now.

This is yet another aspect of your relationship with Me ... My own suffering bringing *you* a sense of serenity.

Simply remain in My love
(John 15:9)

*B*E even more sure of My working when you are blindly trusting and are refusing all impulses to manipulate events yourself.

Helping to make conditions right for Me to bring about My perfect will.

If you are content to act only upon My prompting, then the times of waiting trustingly will be times when peace can descend upon you. Peace in the knowledge that straight away I am bringing some good for you from present circumstances.

Then, as a result of My continual working, an eventual *perfect* solution. My child, can you see My *working* as the secret of being at peace, even at times of great trial?

The water I give you is a well which springs up into eternal life
(John 4:13)

*E*ACH passing minute means that every facet of earth's existence is also passing away.

Be re-assured about the *permanency* of your future if it has been given to Me. Just as the passing of time is inexorable, so are My purposes! Therefore, do not fear what lies ahead. The time which you may now dread is one in which My work for you continues - the shaping of your soul, and My unfailing provision for you.

The refuge of My eternity (*your* refuge) is completely independent of the earthly passage of time. It is here that your soul is kept secure.

**... shall not perish but
have eternal life**
(John 3:16)

*I*F there has been a desperate seeking of My will, I then keep from you everything which would harm, everything which would prevent your receiving what I have in store for you.

There will always be imperfections as you strive to walk in obedience, but I want you to take heart, My child. Take heart because I over-rule those imperfections, and their consequences, where there has been an overall surrender and desire to please Me.

Yes, we *will* conquer together in all situations which you give to Me.

**Be sure to seek first,
the Kingdom of God**
(Matthew 6:33)

*T*RUE worship - either alone or in the company of others - is always the worship of the heart.

Deep thankfulness for My *faithfulness* will always be present in true worship.

And true worship always to be *very* simply expressed...

Contrary to what is so often believed, I accept *all* imperfect devotion. If such devotion, though imperfect, has origins in the heart, it is *made perfect* in My sight.

**To worship in spirit
and in truth**
(John 4:24)

MY child, know that your prayers (so often hesitant or carrying a sense of unworthiness) are always *assisted*.

You have entered the realm of heaven (even though you may not sense this) and My spirit joins with yours to make even the humblest prayer-offering something dear to my heart.

When you have consciously taken Me as your partner, I prosper *only* what is pleasing to Me in what you attempt.

Wherever possible, respond only to very obvious need, as I reveal it to you, leaving other matters safely with Me.

By your love, people will know that you are My disciples
(John 13:35)

*B*E vigilant in recognising attitudes which are plainly not of Me and which may have become habitual:

Are these among them, My child?
...Self-concern in all its forms?
...Discontent?
...Self pity?
...Envy?

Whenever you fall into these things oppose them with what is of Me - especially *gratitude* that in Me you have so much!

Resolutely thank Me for My goodness towards you when events seem to proclaim the opposite. Such gratitude has great power.

**Fix your mind on
God's kingdom**
(Matthew 6:33)

79

$\mathcal{B}$ECAUSE I already see the best possible outcome from every situation of yours, I want you to have more and more of *My* mind.

This means that you will await patiently the sure results of My good influence.

Waiting need not be difficult if you thankfully tell Me that every matter is indeed in My hands. There will then be a growing harmony between your spirit and My own.

I always honour your giving of circumstances to Me by touching the *real* causes of present need.

Yes, My child, answering your prayers in the best possible way.

**Be still before the Lord
and wait patiently for him**
(Psalm 37: 7)

*A*s a light shines out to illuminate dark places, so I become more and more precious to those who reach out to Me - often in prolonged and great need.

Can you see that even the darkest manifestations of earth are not in any way wasted if they compel a child of Mine to single-mindedly seek Me, and then to discover Me as life's priceless gift?

True knowledge of Myself (and especially of My love) is so often rooted in that initial desperate reaching out. I am then encountered as the *supreme contrast* to the darkness of earth.

A pearl of great value
(Matthew 13:46)

I unfailingly lift into My love your burdens of fear and of wrong ways repented over. Simply ask!

The weight of these things is lifted in order that you may go forward once more.

As I lift that burdened spirit into the light of My love, the sheer darkness of your surroundings is less and less able to destroy your peace.

My child, have you learned to give every passing circumstance into My sure hands *as it occurs*? When it is with Me, the circumstance is prevented from further worsening.

Light has come into the world
(John 3:19)

$\mathcal{M}$Y child, the fear of extinction is widespread among mortals; they cannot see beyond the earthly limitations of time, and of the human body.

Let this natural fear be overcome by a sureness that the passing of each day for you, as My chosen, is merely bringing you closer to the delight of My immediate presence!

Your spirit is secure from the natural wasting activity of earth.

I am your great reward
(Genesis 15: 1)

MY child, you realise the value of *prayerful hesitation* before following any road upon which you have decided.

In this way, countless dangers are avoided.

Let there always be peace and clarity before then going forward. Make sure that it is a road over which My light shines.

There is always the temptation to 'reason through' matters which are in My control. Safety consists of abandoning yourself, instead, to *My* solutions.

Trust and expressions of gratitude are all that you will ever really need.

**Do not lean upon
your own understanding**
(Proverbs 3: 5))

*E*VERY worthwhile experience is *enriched* by My presence.

Experiences planned by Me out of loving anticipation... (often to lift you from despair).

The greatest sadness would be if you failed to recognise, and thank Me for, life's most precious experiences.

Such experiences will always be those where the look to My surrounding love carries no jarring note.

...life more abundantly
(John 10:10)

*W*HEN peace temporarily leaves you, remain, consciously, in the shelter of My love, attempting nothing.

The priceless gift of peace will then return deep into your being, as you ensure that I am your only concern.

It is only when peace reigns that you can look upon what is distressing in present concerns as of no *lasting* importance. You are then looking upon the various manifestations of the world with My eye of truth.

Come, and rest for a while
(Mark 6:31)

$\mathcal{A}$LWAYS coming back to My peace in daunting circumstances. So often you will find that your own intervention adds nothing to what I am doing for you.

Because you lack My knowledge, it is a matter of utter trust in My own sure working.

Always *silence* more than controversy or striving, showing how much you rely on My anticipatory work on your behalf.

Therefore, My own unhurried and sure ways to be your pattern.

There is no other Saviour
(Isaiah 43:11)

*I*F, in the very darkest situation, you contemplate My love with all your being, you will always find an opening for *hope* in that situation.

The hope is based, as you know, on the permanency of Myself, contrasted with earth's trials.

Do you realise that it is *impossible* for Me to fail you, even at times when I am hurt by your own failures?

If you really understood My love, you would know that only the deepest sympathy and understanding towards you are possible.

I am the Lord your God ... merciful, gracious, and infinitely patient
(Exodus 34:6)

YES, My child, you *absorb* My love, as you continue to submit gladly to Me and *allow* Me to draw you ever closer.

Let there be a constant *giving* of yourself to Me, and with a feeling of utter security as you do so. This is the only sure remedy for the feelings of solitude or of despair.

Nothing is of more importance than our unity... a unity which is there to draw upon when fear threatens.

A unity which you must always take for granted.

To bear fruit, the branch must stay united with the vine
(John 15:4)

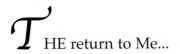

*T*HE return to Me...

...always welcome, with all your being, those times when our communion is restored. Yes, My child, a reflection of My own heart of welcome!

When you are back safely within the peace of My presence: nothing in the world matters at such a time.

Remember that your happiness at the restoration between us can never equal My own.

Happiness that I have brought you home!

**Bring the finest robe,
and put it on him**
(Luke 15:22)

MY child, to follow your heart is always the way of safety. When I see your readiness to obey I will always enlighten - a sure awareness in your heart which must be trusted above all 'reasoning'.

Do not fear about trusting Me in this way! As you follow the peace which accompanies My whisper to your heart you will come to know (even if not always immediately) that you have chosen aright. Yes, My child, never doubt a choice of the heart but, rather, thank Me, trustingly, for the outcome.

The more frequently your heart is followed, the easier you will find it to yield to Me in life's problem-areas, with a sense of My carrying you to avoid the pitfalls laid by evil.

Your heart will be where your treasure is
(Matthew 6:21)

My child, when you are tossed about by circumstances, I know you will remember the one source of stability... the *rock* which is My love for you. Be aware of this steadying factor at all times - one which will never fail you and which will ensure that you are not moved into danger.

Thank Me for the place of safety when all is threatening - ensuring that evil does not beguile you into wrong impulses.

Yes, My child, you are lifted above danger as you cling to Me... never to be moved!

I am with you, wherever you go
(Joshua 1:9)

*A*S you contemplate My love, as you recognise its influence reaching you, you are truly *free* to thank Me and to praise Me to comfort My own heart.

Always I accept your offering in an uncaring and ungrateful world.

My child, I am always deeply grateful when you believe the best of Me... a belief which *always* begins with that inner certainty of My love.

Every word of thanks to Me takes away some of the hurt I experience all the time in a fallen creation.

My joy in them
(John 17:13)

$\mathcal{A}$LWAYS returning quickly to My love, no matter what has gone before! Letting that love *minister to you* as it proves too strong for areas of disturbance.

My love in the foreground of your life is instantly recognised by the forces opposed to Me, which are compelled to retreat. My love has the power to erase, very quickly, the effects of recent distressing experiences.

Harmful distractions are more easily refused as you keep Me in your gaze ... lifted into the realm of light, always a welcoming realm, and one of calm.

I am the bright and morning star
(Revelation 22: 16)

$\mathcal{A}$s you surrender to what I allow you will find that so often this includes:

...Delays
...Disappointments
...Things hard to understand

And yet, let the surrender be accompanied by your gratitude, still, that I am unerringly at work, and with peace in your heart.

As you are learning, I would not permit any circumstance harmful to your eternal destiny.

You can trust My promise that I *will* make all come right, in spite of those things hard to understand.

Rejoice in what I am bringing about for you
(Isaiah 65:18)

*N*EVER will My love be felt by the seeking heart more than when it breaks through to conquer fear and to show that, all the time, you have been benefiting from love's essential *safety*.

Because fear is man's enemy, My anticipation is vital... moulding life's events to buffer what would otherwise cause a loved one a suffering hard to bear.

My child, you are always on safe ground to thank Me for all that I am carrying you through.

Perfect love casts out fear
(1 John: 4: 18)

ONLY by entering a still-developing existence with its many imperfections and dangers could I ensure that My authority was imposed... an existence now bearing the authority of love.

This authority was seen in submission and weakness when I came to your earth, but *always* manifested in the conquest of disease and death.

My child, if only the world could see the *power* of love, even when it seems to have been temporarily defeated.

Yes, in spite of all appearances, love's rule in the universe can always be seen in *My* rule; in lives where I am really trusted.

His power at work within us
(Ephesians 3: 20)

T HERE will be times when everything seems to point away from Me.

And yet your present existence is one in which love is clothed with meaning, and shines in the midst of cruelty, hopelessness and futility.

Even when my light flickers, it will never go out.

Steadfastly making sure that your life's *aim* is fixed keeps the light burning.

The light of my love can never be extinguished by evil's deceptive work. Always ensure that it is *your* light.

The Lord will be your everlasting light
(Isaiah 60: 19)

*E*VEN the *wish* to find Me when darkness is all around, ensures My nearness.

My child, when in darkness, the light will not fail you as you give entrance to it. A gentle light... nevertheless able to scatter fear and any temporary unbelief.

Every single turning to Myself (so often a helpless turning) is a consolidation of our relationship, strengthening the bonds of love between us.

Looking steadfastly, *always,* into the light of My love.

In Him there is no darkness
(1 John 1: 5)

*I*T is against the background of a daunting creation that I can be experienced by the heart reaching out to Me in need.

A child, driven to Myself, finding the only true refuge.

My response to your need is immediate, even when you are not aware of that response.

Simply thank Me, (with that attitude of a rested child) that I am at work for you.

I always reach out, in love, automatically, as a response to your own reaching-out.

'Lord, to whom else can we go?'
(John 6: 68)

*T*HE meaning of My universe is never more clearly seen than when you contemplate My abandonment, in love, to your world at the greatest cost.

Truth is seen only when there is no other *desire* than to see what is of truth. The supreme truth is that My Cross gives creation its meaning.

Can you now see how much is gained by pausing to recall My presence, and by letting the sound of My Name fall upon your inner ear?

You can then deal with life's details with a sureness which is free of haste or agitation.

Only one thing is vital
(Luke 10:42)

*T*HE giving to Me of circumstances which I can use, if given instinctively, always *ensures* My activity on your behalf.

In a real sense, your consenting in faith becomes *part* of that activity - even though you may not be aware of how I am using you.

Always, in My work on your behalf, there is a corresponding work for My kingdom in a wider field beyond yourself.

Imagine how much more quickly My Kingdom would advance if many more of My children invited My working.

**The Lord is faithful
in all He does**
(Psalm 33: 4)

*T*O feel from time to time that you are withdrawing from all the complexities of your existence and, instead, opening yourself to Me.

Here to receive all that is *real* and that which will prove permanent for you.

You learn so much about My nature by My interventions at very crucial points in your life. You learn even more about My love's planning, about My perfect wisdom and attention to detail.

In life's crises, realising, above all, My *faithfulness*.

Surely his goodness and mercy will follow me.
(Psalm 23: 6)

*B*ECAUSE you cannot fully understand existence, you need only see its vastness reflected in an infinity of love.

Error occurs whenever you see My creation as other than founded in love. What you see in your present world is a reflection (on a minute scale) of the greatness of creation.

The one thing which you can really understand and which fills all things, is that universal love. Nothing is more precious to Me than a child I have created.

There is a plan which is beyond your comprehension in which there exists all that is needed to woo the hearts of My children and bring them into the safety of My near presence.

**How wide and deep is
the love of Christ**
(Ephesians 3: 18)

T HOSE who enter any kind of relationship may not realise that there will always be a *building* role, reflecting My own in relation to My world. That role is to redeem the material of the relationship from within.

My child, My Kingdom is built by:

...Every choice which you make
   in harmony with that Kingdom.
...Every word spoken for Me.
...Every invitation for Me to act on
   your behalf.

How important is your own working when it is a prompting of Myself.

God will not forget your work
(Hebrews 6: 10)

*K*EEP a consciousness of My holding you. This is your reminder of the only really safe walk through the hazards always to be encountered

My holding you is especially vital in the *spiritual* hazards of a fallen world.

My child never think of My presence in terms of how close I seem at a given moment. My presence (with My influence exerted upon your life) is *constant*.

As you think of My filling all things you can contemplate fear in the certitude that I will never let you move out of my presence.

**The Lord is my strength
and my shield**
(Psalm 28: 7)

*E*VERY outcome (including that of death itself) is merely a stage in a progression to wholeness for those children putting their trust in Me.

Eventually, all the children of your world will come to know Me as Truth, and find My friendship.

I want you to know that seeming reverses suffered by My cause will not for ever hold up My being revealed as the Saviour of mankind.

The glory of My manifestation will be *unmistakable*.

Every eye shall see Him
(Revelation 1: 7)

*I*T is because everything in the present material existence - including all that is around and within you - is in some way tainted that there must be a constant surrender to My purifying presence.

Whenever you hand everything over to Me you are, in effect, asking that I will strengthen you to do what you could not do for yourself. Needless to say, the strength is automatically there for you.

Yes, My child, surrender, surrender...

Be strong in the Lord
(Ephesians 6: 10)

*A*s you frequently submit the events of life to my working, you are allowing the cosmic power which orders all things to be employed on your behalf - taking away all the strain and effort which accompany self-will.

Efforts to order the details of each day will always be imperfect if I am not consciously involved with you. This is why frequent surrender is so vital. You then become a child who makes it possible for My *sureness* to be there in the midst of complexities.

**We are the clay;
You are the potter**
(Isaiah 64: 8)

*I*T is along the way of submission that, rather surprisingly, you find strength coming.

Your consciousness of human weakness is changed by that submission into an experience of the courage which you need.

My child, receive a most solemn promise as you continue to trust in Me:

...You will see my cause triumph.
...You will see evil defeated.

Yes, believe with all your heart in My *absolute* victory.

Whoever endures to the end will be saved.
(Matthew 24: 13)

MY child, give Me all your love!

You may feel that your love is a poor and variable thing, but simply pour what you have before Me and allow Me to perfect it, holding nothing back. I want you to know the unfailing comfort to My heart as you lay your love before Me.

If it is imperfect love, the *offering* is sufficient because I see your offering unspoiled by your present circumstances or pre-occupations.

I will always remember your offering; it is from this that My provision for you flows (provision which you may not always recognise!)

We love, because he first loved us
(1 John 4: 19)

*I*T is wisdom to focus your mind upon My unchanging love in order to build a spiritual refuge of that love. You then have a place where fear is not able to torture your mind.

The refuge of My love is the only place upon earth which can defeat fear *at its source* - the lying activity of evil.

My child, when you are afraid, stay in the hiding place of My love. See in My countenance that there is nothing but love between us and therefore no room for fear.

Do not be afraid, for I have redeemed you
(Isaiah 43: 1)

*I*T is because of My *mercy* that so many adverse factors in your life (of which you may have no awareness) are brought to nothing.

My child, reflect upon the love which anticipates even your own contrition by continuing to watch over your interests.

My child, do not torture yourself over temporary circumstances. Instead, remember that I am pledged to make everything eventually come into harmony for you.

Once again, it is a question of believing the best of Me!

I will care for you to the end
(Isaiah 46: 4)

*T*HE longer a life deliberately excludes Myself, the greater is the danger to that life.

I want you to believe that love (yes, simply love), has the *power* to rescue. A rescue which I always wish to be permanent, and which establishes Me as Friend.

No trial can be faced successfully with anyone but Myself. My power to overcome resides in My overcoming of evil in all its manifestations (many not seen as having a spiritual source). All this should point you to immediate recourse to Me when you feel unequal to, or frightened by, any disturbance in your life.

With God all things are possible
(Mark 9: 23)

A friendship formed when life is dark for you and the world as a whole seems without meaning.

You will find so often, later, that the sun has indeed been shining upon you because of My working and that your desperate faith has not been in vain.

Whenever you sink into My embracing love, there is no need to tell me any current need.

Just be the child; the essence of our friendship.

Your sun will never set
(Isaiah 60: 19)

MY child, is your steady aim to possess *Me* always?

I am pledged to ensure this for you no matter what you may lose of what the world considers wealth.

However dark life can become, let your quiet prayer be one of gratitude, at all times, that you have the one priceless gift... our *friendship* - never to be broken.

The *grateful* heart is always miracle-working!

I count everything as loss compared with the all-surpassing knowledge of Jesus Christ my Lord
(Philippians 3: 8)

*T*HE greatest of all fears is that of being alone in a friendless existence.

My child, your frequent reaching-out to your Saviour is to ensure your holding on to *life itself* - the life of eternal significance, never to be withdrawn from you.

If you cease all fearful striving and simply allow Me to enfold you (not concerned about feelings) the sense of alone-ness will pass. *My* presence will prove all-sufficient.

An existence friendless no longer!

I have called you friends
(John 15: 15))

$\mathcal{M}$Y child, because my love is above all price, that is why you must never cease diligently to make it your own.

Once found, it is always there to return to should it become temporarily clouded.

If you see love's importance above all else, it will truly become your *life-long possession*.

Ask yourself very frequently how *could* My love fail you?

Being with You, I desire nothing else on earth
(Psalm 73: 25)

M Y child, do not be afraid to face any wrong in your past and present. The courage to face these things comes automatically as you habitually let yourself go in My caressing love.

The sorrow over wrong which My love produces is the *true* sorrow, as opposed to the fearful guilt which is evil's ambition for you.

My child, when you allow My love to bring a true repentance, free from fear, you can be sure that only My love remains between us, and that *all is made right*.

**God is greater
than our hearts!**
(1 John 3: 20)

*W*HEN conscious of failing Me, never believe the lie that because of this My love towards you is even slightly diminished.

The constancy of My love does not depend on your own human efforts. Rather, it depends on your own often-desperate trust in Me, no matter what the circumstances.

My child, from Myself there is *only* an influence of love.

As you welcome that influence, it is all-conquering.

Love never fails
(1 Corinthians 13: 8)

*F*OR a follower of Mine, rescue from what is distressing is never far away. Thank Me in the midst of trials, that I have a place of ease and refreshment already planned for you.

Learn to recognise each little miracle on your behalf.

Never feel that because of your fragility your prayer is not effective. Be content that as you whisper My name you are in My secret place, where I am fully attentive to your need.

He restores my soul
(Psalm 23: 3)

T HERE will be those who have hurt you. But never let your thoughts idly stray into My making people painfully aware of those hurts.

Yes, as I have commanded, pray for such people *with no exceptions.*

Resist all thoughts of ill befalling them.

Only be supremely grateful for:

...The fact that I AM.
...The fact that you *possess* Me.
...The fact that My love for you
    is infinite.

How can *anything* matter compared with these precious truths?

**Pray for those
who persecute you**
(Matthew 5: 44)

MY child, *complete submission to Me* is so important when there is distress of spirit.

Just see My *enfolding* of both yourself and any painful circumstances. This, in itself, prevents further harm, and begins the healing process ... healing of your own spirit and a healing influence upon whatever external factors there may be.

Let there be not the slightest effort of thought during this time of submission of yourself and the emotional needs of the moment to Me. So often My response will have been *in anticipation* of your coming to me!

**Before My children
call I will answer**
(Isaiah 65: 24)

My child, sadness need never lead to complete despair.

Sadness is a sharing of My own heartbrokenness over a fallen world.

But then lift up your head to the light of My resurrection.

Yes, for you there is always the victory of My love over all temporary sadness of heart. Even in sorrow, you can still share with Me My blessings.

If you look earnestly for My love through the clouds of darkness, careful to keep My Name upon your lips, you will always find it.

Your sorrow will be turned into joy
(John 16: 20)

$\mathcal{M}$Y child, you must realise that if you spend much time absorbing My love, you are *made strong*.

This is one of the many changes in you which living in My love brings about. You then confront situations with the ability to overcome taken for granted. Yes, using what is yours, rather than seeking desperately for strength.

The principal challenges for My followers are: the overcoming of temptation and wrongdoing, the overcoming of ways of weakness and (very importantly) the over coming of fear.

Simply believe that for the demands of life you have become a stronger person... just by living with Me.

Whoever overcomes will inherit all things
(Revelation 21: 7)

*T*HE walk in My way becomes more and more full of delights if only you will look away resolutely from every jarring factor.

Yes, delights through the medium of the world but indwelt by Myself.

Frequently speaking My Name will help you more readily to find joy in so many commonplace things as I lift you above them, and meet with you.

Therefore, My child, do not flee the world, but be content to be immersed in it, knowing that increasingly you will encounter Me there!

No-one will be able to take your joy from you
(John 16: 22)

T HE setting for My manifestation to the earth is one of human
struggle, much imperfection and
apparent blind chaos.

My creative work is concerned with
redeeming all phenomena and
enabling love to be seen, eventually,
as My unchanging purpose.

My child, if I am *allowed* to do so, I
will always redeem the chaos of
your own personal environment.
I will bring meaning into the
complexities. I will ensure that My
love is not only seen by you but
that it shines through you.

What I do in your own situation will
contribute to the manifestation of
Myself for the whole earth.

God said 'Let there be light...'
(Genesis 1: 3)

$\mathcal{B}$EFORE you make decisions of a practical nature, ensure that My peace is there! The presence of My peace will bring about for you what other agencies or remedies can only partially achieve.

Do you realise, My child, that when, in uncertainty, you speak My name and let everything go into My love, you have made the *major* decision?

The major decision is *allowing* Me, by your trust, to bring about what is right (when you cannot, for the moment, see the way forward).

I will always prompt and strengthen you concerning any needed action of your own, but the vital factor is, at all times, *My* working.

Following Me you will never walk in darkness
(John 8: 12)

MY child, you will have discovered from My words to you, that refusing all troubling of the spirit needs to be *immediate*.

Let the thought of My love be uppermost, let it be *all*, as I take all anxiety and fret into that love.

Surrendering to My love, you can then be sure of My working in all things for your good. This is so that you may indeed be unburdened!

You will find, in all aspects of life, that nothing is asked of you except that child-like surrender of yourself into My arms.

My child, the frequent whispering to Me of 'Only *You*, Lord' and 'Only Your Love'.

He is my refuge and my fortress
(Psalm 91: 2)

*I*F your feelings do not always reassure you of My presence, I want you to *remember* all that I have done on your behalf.

My interventions for you, always independent of any other agency, are all part of miracle work, and to remember them gratefully will help to restore your faith when it wavers.

In response to your child-like trust I am constantly stepping into your circumstances. This will so often be in the seemingly small details.

Learn to notice My interventions each day as I turn to good so many seemingly impossible situations. Your gratitude will both keep hope alive and comfort My own heart.

Praise the Lord, O my soul and do not forget all His benefits
(Psalm 103: 2)

MY child, it will always bring you peace when you *contrast* the changes in earthly circumstances with My unchanging love.

Learn to accept that circumstances on earth can never be perfect and then, consolidate your relationship with Me, so that My love is victorious in *any* situation.

So much that happens to you in your world is out of your direct control and it is folly to try to change circumstances with haste or vain persuasion.

Earth's fret-producing fortunes are, of course, a burden upon you *unless* you learn thankfully to surrender them. Yes, My child, never expect too much of what is in your world, but expect more and more of *Me!*

As for God, His way is perfect
(Psalm 18: 30)

*E*VEN when, on the earthly level, there are unsolved difficulties, and many things to be 'made right', you can *still* experience rest for your soul!

My child I want you to covet the great gift of enjoying rest of soul in spite of the world's intrusions.

When you look away to My love in the midst of anxieties of various kinds, I reward that look by ensuring My peace for you.

Even in the darkest circumstances you can find a *poise* which speaks of My presence with you. A poise which could only come from trusting My love.

He is our peace
(Ephesians 2: 14)

*T*HE world's inscrutability is very deliberately so. The riddle of creation makes the sense of My nearness, given to the trusting heart, all the more precious.

In making your way through the present world, with your life given to Me, certainty grows about the one thing which matters - My unfailing love.

To know fear in an existence which is often threatening is a very natural thing. But I stand guard, ready to take from you the burden of fear, whenever you simply throw yourself upon My love.

When I am afraid,
I will trust in You
(Psalm 56:3)

$\mathcal{N}$EVER, believe the lie, implanted by evil, that there is serious risk in leaving a matter entirely to My working.

It is because My ways are sure that you need have no fear concerning anything which you entrust to Me.

My child, will you ensure these two main aspects of your walk with Me?:

...Firstly, the surrender to Me of all which is 'beyond you' (those things with which you feel powerless to deal).

...Secondly, remembering the imperative of using My strength to patiently carry out what I enable you to do.

His incomparably great power
(Ephesians 9: 19)

MY child, have you considered the environment into which you come with your burdens? You are bringing them into the place of My love!

It is here, in the divine refuge, that you become aware of My constant readiness to take to Myself whatever troubles you.

Yes, even before you lay before Me your specific burdens of fear, anxiety, guilt, difficult decisions, sad memories, you can feel something of the peace which comes simply from being *with Me* in that refuge.

Thank Me, often, for the victory of My love.

**The Lord is my helper;
I will not be afraid**
(Hebrews 13: 6)

A misguided concept of an implacable divine justice has caused many to be in fear of approaching Me.

My child, because My nature is essentially one of tender mercy. I *always* respond to the trembling or the penitent heart. I am infinitely sad when a burden remains and the torture of self-blame continues.

So many of My children would have gone away with their burdens unrelieved if they had not believed, warmly, that the Saviour of the world was 'meek and lowly of heart'.

Cast your burden upon the Lord
(Psalm 55: 22)

*T*HE Cross gives to the world a very clear message of *freedom* for all who surrender to the love shown.

My child, does the sight of My suffering love arouse your pity? Let it also give you a boldness to lay down all that weighs heavily upon you. Just let me, from the Cross, take these things into My heart.

As you surrender to My love there, the Cross becomes a place of victory for you. Those forces seeking to destroy you are brought to nothing in their designs upon your life.

By His wounds we are healed
(Isaiah 53: 5)

MY child, the way simply has to be narrow!

The way was planned to ensure your eventual arrival at your eternal home.

How easy it is to wander into by-paths! Along these by-paths there can be fierce temptations (not at first apparent to you). Therefore, to tread the narrow way, just keep Me as the home of your thoughts, and allow Me to complete all your efforts.

My child, a seemingly hard way, but it is the way of *harmony*, along which I give you a priceless sense of security.

The road which leads to life is a narrow one
(Matthew 7: 14)

$\mathcal{M}$Y child, your human nature is so designed that it has constant need of Me!

The spiritual side of your being is of the utmost importance and there is danger when you neglect it.

Your human nature is not functioning as it was meant to do when the strength and grace which I give are not used. One then becomes an unbalanced person.

In order to survive in the world's difficult places you need to feel 'at home' with Me... becoming what you were created to be.

...in My own likeness
(Genesis 1: 26)

γOU will often encounter those who are burdened in spirit.

As you try to help in some way, ask Me to give you what to say to them, so that, through your prayer, their burdens may be lifted.

When someone finds relief from what has been troubling them (often something of long standing), this is a clear sign that I have been at work.

Always tell the person that I am answering prayer for them; this brings glory to My name.

My child... our *partnership*!

Serve the Lord with all your heart
(Isaiah 12: 20)

WITHOUT the assurance that I will always go ahead of you to provide and protect, life's many demands would overwhelm you.

Are there times when you face many demands upon you? I want you to take time to *survey each demand singly*. Then thank Me that each one will be under My good influence.

So often My children have been amazed (looking back on things which seemed to threaten) to see how they have safely negotiated those things about which they prayed.

**I will go with you,
and prosper all that you do**
(Exodus 33: 14)

MY child, frequently contrast the fickleness of this world with divine faithfulness.

Yours is the privilege of standing upon solid ground when all around is of change and confusion.

Upon that solid ground you will always find a strengthening which you may not find in your natural self.

Courage may not always be easy for you, but it will be there to steady you at any time that you dwell upon My *faithfulness*.

I will be with you when you go through deep waters
(Isaiah 43: 2)

MY child, think of how great is your satisfaction when you can ease the burden of a fellow human being.

You can then understand My great joy when I am allowed to take from *you* all that is burdensome.

Remember that as I bear sorrow and pain for you, it always ministers to My own heart.

When you express your gratitude to Me for sharing your burdens, it shows Me that My choosing of you was not in vain!

The Lord will delight in you
(Isaiah 62: 4)

MY child, do you realise that to *worship* Me is essential to your progress in the spiritual realm?

Two vital aspects of worship are:

...The praise of a *grateful* heart.
...The renewing of your spirit.

So many of the miracles for which you long will occur in answer to your expressions of worship.

The worship of My children so often comes from sad hearts. And yet that sad heart can also be a thankful heart! A heart which remembers many blessings and times of rescue.

Worship the Lord with gladness
(Psalm 100: 2)

*T*HE storms of life will take many forms:

...Someone's anger with you.
...Someone's unjust criticism.
...Someone's almost deliberate misunderstanding.
...Someone's lack of sympathy.

My child, *any* disturbance, *any* ruffling of the spirit can only remain if you forget to turn to Me as your shield.

Whatever may be happening around you, remember to speak quietly My Name in defiance of the storm. The storm has always to subside in the face of that Name, and you will be able to watch it do so.

**The storm subsided
and all was calm**
(Luke 8: 24)

My child, you are learning that there is so much danger in attempting to live without Me.

It is vital to allow every detail of life (even the most seemingly trivial), to be approached with a consciousness of our unity.

Yes, there is only one really safe place in an increasingly complex existence... that of being (through your own choice), in My arms of love.

Is this *your* constant choice?

Without Me you are completely unprepared for the lures and vexations of this present world.

Keep yourselves in the love of God
(Jude 21)

'SELF-RELIANCE' takes on an entirely new meaning if you are My follower.

True self-reliance is trust in what you are able to do, having become strong simply by being united with Me.

Yes, this new and stronger person (you) can be *relied upon* because it is, in effect, reliance upon Me.

Your confidence grows as you think of yourself as this new person, able to face, with courage, the world's challenges.

Self-reliant in the best-sense of the word!

Partakers of the divine nature
(2 Peter 1: 4)

*T*HE reason for My entering the historical process was not merely to reveal My divinity unmistakably.

My incarnation was in order that *love* should become victorious over the many manifestations of evil which spoil the lives of My children.

Underlying My invitation 'Come to Me' was My overall mission to heal the broken-hearted and to release those who are bound in various ways. A mission not to condemn but to save.

As I lift your burdens, think of My joy at seeing that mission of love working in a child's life (yours).

Loved with an everlasting love
(Jeremiah 31: 3)

*A*s you walk through this present world always keep a sense of 'the two of us'. Keep this sense in the midst of all other relationships and casual meetings.

The unity of a child and its Saviour is a fortress against all kinds of unseen dangers.

Let our unity bring an assurance of peace, which contrasts with the frequently-strident character of your surroundings.

Our unity is one which can remove all obstacles and bring you so many victories.

Set your mind on things above
(Colossians 3: 2)

*T*HE light of heaven... this light shines around you as My trusting child!

The divine light make powerless those forces opposed to Me.

With My light around you, you are enabled to see the truth about the various worldly phenomena.

It is heaven's light into which your burdens are lifted, enabling you to go on your way with a sense of freedom.

As you desire Me, above all, heaven's light will always accompany you.

Let us walk in the light of the Lord
(Isaiah 2: 5)

$\mathcal{R}$EMEMBER that I *go before you* into those occasions which cause you apprehension. Always give those occasions to Me in utter trust.

As I go before you, you will see that the strength needed to meet circumstances which you find challenge or daunting, will often surprise you!

Yes, My child, the secret lies in what we confront *together*.

Be comforted in that I am already in that future occasion which you may dread, preparing an answer for you.

He will watch over your life
(Psalm 121: 7)

*H*OW limited is the reassurance given by even the kindest and wisest of earthly friends...

Sadly, if you seek this reassurance without Myself involved, your burdens will remain.

Mankind's burdens are the result of the deceptions of the powers of darkness, and that is why *only* the divine power can successfully confront this activity in a human heart.

In response to your believing the best of Me, a wonderful sense of relief from burdens is given, which nothing else could bring about.

The Lord sets the prisoners free
(Psalm 146: 7)

*T*HE burden of guilt is always one of the hardest to bear.

My child, the divine justice is always tempered by love and understanding. Judging yourself harshly is contrary to My purposes for your life.

When you come to Me in penitence it is a *welcoming* presence to which you come. The very fact of your turning to Me for the relief of your burdens shows Me that true penitence is present.

You simply cannot exhaust My patience, which is a facet of My unchanging love!

I uplift the penitent ones
(Isaiah 57:15)

*T*O tread My narrow road is, in effect, making room for My working upon life's details, eliminating all that would be wasteful and which could not carry My blessing.

Along My way I allow *only* those meetings with people which can serve My purposes for your life. Therefore, you can thank Me for all that I allow... even if you do not see its significance immediately.

My child, along the narrow way, all is being made right for you and you will never regret embarking upon My road to life.

Take My yoke upon you
(Matthew 11: 29)

*W*HENEVER you feel prompted to do a kindness (raising someone's morale) remember that the prompting is Mine, and that I also indwell the recipient!

Yes, My child, there are always two who receive from you in an act of love and consideration... Myself and a child of Mine.

There are many ways of ministering to My heart - either in your worship or in your acts of obedience.

My Kingdom is unfailingly extended whenever light shines - even momentarily - in someone's darkness.

...you did it unto Me
(Matthew 25:40)

*M*Y child, think of all that is yours if you possess Me - the one priceless gift.

You have something after which men strive but which so often eludes them... true peace of heart and mind.

You have a covering of love which keeps you from so many subtle worldly intrusions.

You have a presence which draws to you those of My children who can act (as from Me) for your benefit.

You have, of course, the sure hope of eternal life which anything promised by mankind can never equal.

I am the wealth which you need
(Numbers 18: 20)

$\mathcal{A}$S I have told you, there are so many blessings upon the narrow way. Treading that way, I shield you from the very worst of earth's suffering (a shielding so often unknown to you).

Upon that way, I use your life as an offering for the sufferings of others.

Upon that way, there will be countless instances of My breaking into life for you to bless you and to smooth your path.

My child, thank Me for keeping you from harm upon that way.

Especially do I desire to keep from you all that would take you away from Me.

I am with you always
(Matthew 28: 20)

*A*s we negotiate the narrow way (always *assisted*), you will find that the sense of being carried is no illusion but, rather, the experience of all who truly hide themselves in Me.

Along that way I teach you many advantageous lessons and turn to good countless 'misfortunes'. I give Myself to others through you - often in the most unlikely situations.

I safely bring you through so many *hidden* dangers and help you to recognise at once when you are straying from that way.

Yes, My child, I repeat My assurance: the narrow way is always the *easiest* way.

He will not let your foot be moved
(Psalm 121: 3)

*M*Y child, the future holds so much which would cause you dread.

At the heart of these things are the *ultimate* fears - of death itself, and of the bitter disappointment of finding that life is empty of meaning after all.

Resolutely see the unknown surrounded by My love; see the darkness lit by it.

Move into the unknown with a courage born of trust that My love is all that matters.

To be with Me where I am and to see My glory
(John 17:24)

MY child, can you see that everything you endure *with Me* helps to build a wonderful inheritance for you?

That inheritance will be to find true contentment in My love.

Yes, a measure of that divine contentment will be experienced, at first, in your present world, where so much is adverse.

Rejoice that no-one can take away your inheritance because it is grounded in My eternity.

Come, you blessed of My Father
(Matthew 25: 34)

REMEMER that all that *really* matters is what I have in My hands for you.

Therefore, see what I am now doing for you in the light of what My love has fashioned for you in eternity.

See all that you have endured, as well as My provision and protection through the years, as all part of My preparation-work.

Yes, you are being made ready for an existence of real meaning at last.

The only thing which will be unchanged in that existence is, of course, My love for you!

I chose you ...
(John 15:16)

*W*HEN you feel that all is lost, this is the very time when I am sure to come to your aid in a special way.

I come as you fly to My loving embrace.

It is in this embrace that you slowly discover that all is not really lost! You find that hope can never be completely destroyed.

And you will have made a Friend, amidst all those earthly misfortunes. It is this Friend who takes your hand and leads you to a place where you find that the good news of My love is not too good to be true, after all.

I will give the fountain of the water of life
(Revelation 21:6)

My child, My sharing will never come to an end.

I wait longingly to see your own joy at eventually attaining My near presence.

It will be a joy shared, first of all, by just one other... Myself!

**So that your joy
may be complete**
(John 15:24)

I AM WITH YOU

DIVINE HELP FOR TODAY'S NEEDS
New and amplified edition
of the well-loved modern
devotional classic

FR JOHN WOOLLEY

Words taken from 'I Am With You' page one:

I am the hope of all the ends of the earth. But so few truly know it deep in their hearts. In Me lies the fulfilment of the complex desires and possibilities of human nature.

You know that all the qualities you see in Me are available for you. Are you sad, My child, that so often you fail to make use of them? Yes, this is the world's failing - that men do not appropriate that which is there for them, in Me.

Set Me before you always as your one true hope. Be sure that your hand is firmly in Mine ... Proclaim Me as mankind's hope to those around you ... As you recognise the progress you make with Me, so the conviction will grow which you bring to telling others, all that I can be to them!

I know that in your heart is that longing to know Me more perfectly. I honour that longing, and that is why you are sure of My patience in all your failures. It is, of course, My grace which helps you to maintain that longing - and to come, increasingly, into oneness with Myself.

**I will never turn away anyone
who comes to Me**
(John 6: 37)

I AM WITH YOU

These are some examples of the high praise received for *I Am With You* (companion volume to *My burden is Light*):

I Am With You will bring peace and consolation to all who read it.'   *Cardinal Murphy-O'Connor*
former Archbishop of Westminster

'A very special book, which will bless countless people.'   *Prebendary John Pearce*
in the Church of England Newspaper

'A lovely book of devotions. We use it daily.'
Dr. Donald English
former President, Methodist Conference

'*I Am With You*' is a little gem.'   *Joyce Huggett*
Author

THE "I AM WITH YOU" FELLOWSHIP

Readers of Fr John's inspired words may join the
I Am With You Fellowship. All in the Fellowship
are remembered in prayer and are encouraged to
write about any particular need. To join, please send
your name, address (incl. postcode), phone number
and email address (if available) to:-

I Am With You Foundation
c/o Goodnews Books, Upper Level,
St John the Apostle Church Complex,
296 Sundon Park Road,
Luton, Beds, LU3 3AL
01582 571011
email: orders@goodnewsbooks.net
www.goodnewsbooks.net

The Fellowship distributes mini copies of
John Woolleys books free of charge all over the world.
If you would like to make a donation in support of this
work please send it to:-

I Am With You Foundation
2 Lauradale Road
London N2 9LU, UK
Tel 0208 883 2665
Email:- contact@iamwithyou.co.uk

For further information, please visit our website:-
www.iamwithyou.co.uk

Further copies of this book
and other books by Fr. John Woolley

I Am With You

Many Mansions

Abide in My Love

I Am With You for Young People

are available by mail order
and on the internet from:

Goodnews Books
Upper Level, St. John's Church Complex,
296 Sundon Park Road, Luton, Beds.,
LU4 9HG, UK   Tel: 01582 571011
or on the secure web site:
www.goodnewsbooks.net